THE WELL SPEAKS OF ITS OWN POISON

The Dorset Prize

MAGGIE SMITH

THE WELL SPEAKS OF ITS OWN POISON

POEMS

TUPELO PRESS

North Adams, Massachusetts

Library of Congress Cataloging-in-Publication Data

Smith, Maggie, 1977–
 [Poems. Selections]
 The well speaks of its own poison : poems / Maggie Smith. -- First paperback edition.
  pages ; cm. -- (The Dorset prize)
 ISBN 978-1-936797-56-1 (softcover : acid-free paper)
 I. Title.
 PS3619.M5918A6 2015
 811'.6--dc23
                    2014047380

First paperback edition: April 1, 2015.

Cover and text designed by Ann Aspell in Adobe Garamiond and Diotima.
Cover art: Su Blackwell, "The Woodcutter's Hut" (2008), book-cut sculpture with lights, 230
mm D x 310 mm W x 180 mm H. Copyright © 2014 Su Blackwell (www.sublackwell.co.uk).
Used with permission.

Epigraphs used in this book come from the following sources: Amy Gerstler, "Russian Lullaby"
(*Bitter Angel*, North Point Press, 1990); Beckian Fritz Goldberg, "Washed in the River" (*The
Book of Accident*, University of Akron Press, 2006); Brigit Pegeen Kelly, "Dead Doe" (*Song*, BOA
Editions, 1995); Larry Levis, "The Two Trees" (*The Selected Levis*, University of Pittsburgh Press,
2003); William Matthews, "A Happy Childhood" (*Selected Poems and Translations, 1969–1991*,
Mariner, 1992); Mark Strand, "The Dress" (*Darker*, Atheneum, 1970); Terese Svoboda, "Bridge,
Mother" (*Treason*, Zoo Press, 2003).

TUPELO PRESS
P.O. Box 1767, North Adams, Massachusetts 01247
Telephone: (413) 664–9611 / editor@tupelopress.org / www.tupelopress.org

Tupelo Press is an award-winning independent literary press that publishes fine fiction, nonfic-
tion, and poetry in books that are a joy to hold as well as read. Tupelo Press is a registered
501(c)(3) nonprofit organization, and we rely on public support to carry out our mission of
publishing extraordinary work that may be outside the realm of the large commercial publishers.
Financial donations are welcome and are tax deductible.

for VIOLET AND RHETT

CONTENTS

2.

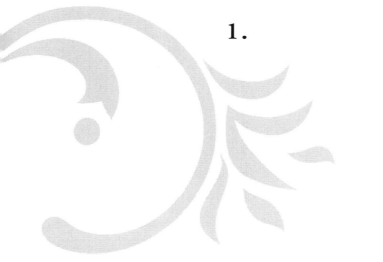

1.

Child. We are done for
in the most remarkable ways.

—Brigit Pegeen Kelly

Vanishing Point

When she leaves the path, the forest opens for her
like a picture book minus the story in which
she has a deer for a brother and braids him a leash
out of flowers. It's no way to live. The girl does not know
wickedness when she sees it. What is she doing alone?
Gathering nosegays? Using her mother's disregard
to hack through the brambles? She measures her distance
in lines: a sonnet for every fourteen steps down
a long hall of yellow leaves. They smell bitter as aspirin.
In the nearly invisible rain, they twitch as if tugged
by clear wires. What a pity, she never arrives.
For all she knows, the woman still waits for wine
and cake, her gown gathering dust from the sands
of ancient Egypt, from stars burnt out a billion years ago.
The girl is lost, not hunted. Taken, but not into a hot,
dark mouth. Nothing lurks in the fir's blue pins.
Swallowed whole by trees, eaten alive in a manner
of speaking, she walks toward a point none of us can see.
It is blacker there than in the gut. From far off, her life
rings like a thrown voice. Let it not be a fable for others.

APOLOGUE (I)

En la tierra del olvido, donde de nada nadie se acuerda...

In the land where all is forgotten, where no one remembers anything,
birds cut off their beaks to share your sorrow, Little Torn Shoe.
Twice of half a moon throbbed, swollen. I don't know what
you mourned. This tale was lost among the chestnut trees,
where I found it and brought it to you. Little Bird of Many Colors,
you are the kind who confuses wondering with wandering.
You wonder around. Under your braids, a bright light.
Little Pink Apple, life does not taste as good as it should.
After all, there is always something better. We choose the best
of what is before us, but much is not before us. In the story,
a boy chose the horse called Thought over the one called Wind.
Thinking swiftly, he rode to you. His sack of apples turned
to a sack of rats; his sack of pears to parrots repeating
happy, happy, happy... Little Gold Pin, many things we tell
our children are kind but not true. The reverse is also true.
You were crying in the chestnut trees. There was no telling
the leaves from the leaf-shaped spaces between them.
I don't know what you mourned, Little Winter Deer, the birds
mute and bleeding all around you. I know you want to forget
that last part. *And here a cup got broken. Everyone should now go home.*

Wren Songs

It's an installation: Wrens pinned like brooches
to the trees, singing, their eyes glass beads.

Shake a branch, be wary of what falls.

In the unofficial spring, sunshine plays xylophone
on the lawn. The trebly notes are mouths

singing *oh, oh, oh*. A paper boat leads

the children downstream, through countless
shades of green—spring, grass, moss, forest.

Light plus one green makes another.

The exhibit rotates seasonally. Soon enough
the children will instead be foxes, the greens

will rust. Someone will strike the wren set.

But for now their songs saturate the air.
If the message is urgent, they'll tell again tomorrow.

The List of Dangers

The black windows looked out onto the black lawn.
—Larry Levis

No one except the three daughters checked off
    the list of dangers. It was like when the wolf ate
        chalk to soften his voice, but the white goats

knew him by his black paws. They filled his gut
    with stones and led him to water so black, it erased
        itself from photographs. No one except the three

knew of hidden rooms in the forsythia, a brittle nest
    for curling into when the neighbor boys chased them
        through the yards. It was not a list of dangers,

but fears. Their father said they had to leave.
    There would be no more safe enclosures.
        No door of yellow, star-shaped flowers.

There were black boys in the city. They would be
    waiting when the girls stepped off the school bus.
        White flight, thought the daughters, as they fled

down a corridor of blossoming pear trees. A child
    crossing the street repeated, *Red hand changes*
        to white man walking. The sun was a saw blade,

a yellow circle with teeth. Terrible birds with plumage
    of fire scorched whatever they touched: The black
        mailbox opened its mouth to the black street.

The daughters checked them off. It was more than a list.
Each *X* clicked like a typewriter key, imprinting the sleep
of those who still slept. Nothing stays good for long—

not the new neighborhood with its wrist full of charms,
not the last tier of wedding cake in the icebox, white
and glittering like a glacier. No one was preserved,

an heirloom apple. Not even the three daughters
would taste exactly as girls did hundreds of years ago.

RED DELICIOUS

Because her knees were already scarred
shiny and pink, the first daughter was sent

into the apple trees. She was perfect
for the task, face already scraped

by what could have been a tree branch
but was not. Each fist of fruit wanted

to stay put, but she twisted it free:
Rome, Jonathan, Golden and Red

Delicious. No one delivered the firstborn,
the tomboy, from the orchard's neat rows.

She was not the beautiful daughter,
but there would be others for beauty.

Because she shinnied up the trees,
others could wait below with bushel sacks.

Because she'd already been bruised,
she was the only one in the trees.

She swung in the sun-fluttered leaves.
She unscrewed apples from their stems,

taking her time because her small hands
were strong, and she let them fall.

OHIO

Ohio, Ohio, Ohio. Often I sing
to myself all day…
—WILLIAM MATTHEWS

The landscape sings in you like a dial tone,
flat and constant: a trick of patience.
But your own voice rasps, always

on the verge of breaking. Here the trees'
shadows slant so crisp on the lawn,
you can walk the branches, veins

in a papery eyelid. You can climb without
leaving the ground. Clots of sunlight
are like nests in these branches,

assembled rather than deposited. Listen
as bird songs repeat, records skipping:
Ohio, Ohio, Ohio. Each persistent

melody chips away at the air, shaving
the sky into tissue-thin curls that float
down like leaves. Like a moat of lilacs

and lambs' ears, the garden circled
your house. You pinched snapdragons
to make them mouth your words

and ate berries that stung your mouth;
a little poison would strengthen
and sing in you. All light was

piecemeal. Your shadow was so tall,
sometimes it escaped you. Riding home
from Sequoia Pool in the family

Volkswagen, you and your sisters
peeled your thighs from the backseat's
hot vinyl. The seatbelt buckle branded

its open mouth into your waist.
That burning was a song: *Ohio, Ohio,
Ohio.* As a child you drew yourself

inverted, with skin on the inside
and organs arranged all over you
like refrigerator magnets: red ovals,

circles, coils. Vulnerability can turn
a body inside out. This is what no one
tells you. Remember "Für Elise" muffled

in the evenings, your sister's foot
on the piano pedal. The television
muttering its litany of commercials,

your mother's velour robe buzzing
and snapping with static. Next door
the neighbors' dog barked incessantly,

the looping soundtrack of the cul-de-sac
where you rode your banana-seat bike
in figure eights. Like a nest, memory

is assembled. You imagined that you
were born from no one, belonging only
to yourself. Once you stayed up late

to watch the sun materialize like credits
at the end of a film. When your breath
vanished from the glass, it was as if

you'd never stood there, planting
your cloudy kiss on the window.
Its edges closed in, a trick of patience.

This is what no one tells you. This place
raised you as one of its own: blue as ink
and almost as useful; sturdy and good

with your hands. But there's darkness
you've never seen, not even through
your eyelids. A piecemeal light

clothes everything in scraps. *Ohio, Ohio,
Ohio:* flat and constant as a dial tone,
it sings in you. It verges on breaking.

Freedom Colony

The moon was a parade float,
the crickets played a bad cover of a song,
and the neighborhood streets were named
for the American Revolution: Lexington,
Valley Forge, Bunker Hill. But the kids
named the cul-de-sacs: Summer Darkness,
The Bicycles, Our Hands Held Before Us.
A harmonica wheezing on the air knew
where it was coming from. On Liberty,
the view from my bedroom obscured
by a pine. Stone geese in yellow rain slickers.
Mailboxes stuffed with my babysitting flyers.
One father took me home late. We sat
idling in the drive, his hand on my thigh.
I had to close my eyes to hear "Blue Bayou."
Opening them, I could see my window.
Through the sticky lace of pine branches,
the moon float made entirely of flowers.

APOLOGUE (2)

Y no miento. Yo no estaba, pero dicen los que lo vieron…

I cannot lie. I wasn't there, **but** *those who saw it say*
you crossed the fields, holding a feather like a torch
to light your way. Little Night Bloomer, it was late.
A child no one looked after was still swinging like a stone
in a slingshot. Her voice carried, so in a way she was many
places at once. Little Bead of Mercury, the firebird prickled
where his feather had been. Because it was not yours
to pluck, he cursed your search for a wife. In the story,
she rose into the spiced air, a star set deep in her forehead
like a jewel. Why this one, when so many maidens spring
from the flesh of oranges? Little Horse of Seven Colors,
the devil used your luck to pick his teeth. It was too late
in the quilt of fields, in the chapel, even for the voices
of children. Your wife covered her body with feathers
instead of a wedding gown. Little Gilded Key, what kind
of bride disguises herself as a rare bird? I don't know
what became of this union. I lost the story before
it ended, Little Thief of Light. It was torn from my hands.
This is true. The wind carried it away and left it on the high sea.

An Island in the Movies

And though only children were meant
to believe this, I still believe this.
                    —Beckian Fritz Goldberg

I packed my sister's suitcase by putting an idea
in her head—that at the other end of the sewer pipe

waited the world we had before the child bride
disappeared from bed, before razorblades

in apples and boys no older than the ones
on our street dying far away, alone, and piled up

on the news. I wanted to believe that I sent her
like a scout, and she'd come back for the rest of us.

My sister crawled inside, and the darkness sort of
ate her. At least that's how I remember it—

like looking at a photograph and knowing someone
is just outside the edges. When she stopped

calling *Polo*, I ran home and said I hadn't seen her
since breakfast, that she was up a tree

or on the Albrights' trampoline. I wanted to believe
the fable I told myself—that the missing and dead

were together somewhere, like an island in the movies,
with no phones for telling us they're all right,

and no boats or planes to bring them home.
That she crawled toward a pinhole of pink-gold light

and waves like applause. That what I'd promised
was real: a place where everyone wears palm leaves,

and blue-and-yellow parrots eat right from your hand.

SPARROW SONGS

Ticking in the trees all around us, white-throated
sparrows are alarms set for the predawn hours.
They play on a loop, frantic. *O sweet Clementine,*

Clementine, Clementine. There is no one

who can turn them off. I cover my ears with shells.
Inside some, the sea plays backwards and sounds
more like the sky. But I can hardly hear it over

the sparrow alarm. That must mean

it's time for something. Every morning
they tell us the same thing, but there is no one
to translate. I have shells for ears, but I can't hear

their scratchy recordings of the sea's

live song skipping *wave, wave, wave.* Like tiny machines,
the sparrows print their messages over and over
on the air scrolling by. Now the words must be

everywhere. We must be breathing them.

MENTAL NOTE

It is so early. The school buses are talking.
All night, cars drove lights across the wall,
the shapes interrupting my sleep. My dreams
are so obvious, they condescend.
For example, last night I wore a sweater
monogrammed with someone else's initials.
I mime writing this with an invisible pen
on my left palm. Mark this spot or turn
down the page—you'll want to come back here.
Sometimes you wear the name of a stranger
as your own. You swerve the car to avoid
the shadow of a bird on the street. It is so early.
Is that a window or a snapshot of a window
projected on the wall? My head rings
maybe, maybe like a French telephone.
Outside, the robotic voice of a school bus
herds children safely onto the sidewalk.
Please step away from the school bus.
The school bus is about to move.

Notes on Camp

The boys' cabins are named for Indian Tribes,
ours for suffragettes. On the rifle range, we lie

in sniper position and shoot watermelons.
Every year it's the same. Archery, canoeing,

model rocketry, and one Cheyenne who claims
he's frenched an Elizabeth Cady Stanton.

The Homesick Girls are in their bunks
in Susan B. Anthony, sniffling, writing pink

letters. *Please come get us. We hate it here.*
At the Camp Show I sing all the vowels

in "Twinkle, Twinkle, Little Star." After lights out,
the Apaches and Alice Pauls meet on the dock

and wait for Turtleman to walk out of the lake
covered in algae, his ghost shoes squishing.

In the Lucy Burns bathroom, we crowd around
the mirror and chant *Bloody Mary* forty times.

They say if you pretend to cradle her baby,
you'll see it dead in your arms, but the séance

never works. It won't work next year either.
That's camp. If everything changed, I wouldn't

come back. Each night the Homesick Girls shine
flashlights under the covers and scribble

pleas in that weird glow. But no one's coming
for them, not even Turtleman. No one ever does.

GAME

Before I saw camouflage painted
with blood, I saw the gutted deer
hanging from a tree in the yard,
his tongue lolling to one side,
back hooves barely grazing the grass.
I had to pose with him in a photograph,
sort of smiling beside the gaping seam
running the length of his belly.
He was not a doll that lost its stuffing,
not a hollowed canoe for sailing
down the creek to wherever it led,
not a new room, not a body I could wear
like a puppet. What little I could see
inside was dark, sticky, smelling of rust.
Where did all the slick, pink organs go?
I never asked. But like the cut
branches and raked leaves, they were
likely tossed into the creek and cleansed
in the water downstream, wherever it led.
My father left the eyes for photographs.
They were already going stale,
then were replaced with shinier ones,
dolls' eyes that never turn to Xs,
never shrivel, never see. It hurts me
to think I imagined his body as a place
to hide from the sight of him.

Apologue (3)

Para saber y contar y contar para aprender…

*To know in order to tell **and** to tell in order to know,*
Little Song of a Strange **Bird**, this is the story as I know it.
Inside each tree you open, a room. Inside each room,
a white bed. But who can sleep with lies chattering
in the drapes like trapped birds? You have the eyes
of a cat and claws beneath your opera gloves. Little Blood
Cordial, do you know what you are? Too many times
you've tried to pass as a cup of honey. You drink wine
from a hollowed horse hoof. Little Kettle of Lye among
Cakes of Soap, the spell's supposed to fill your cupboards
with clove-studded oranges and apples, always apples.
If I were you, I wouldn't eat them; poison has a way
of finding its maker. Little Whisker on a Witch's Chin,
I don't know what's underneath your bearskin cape,
your goat-hair wig. The look in your eyes isn't human.
But it's not too late. Even a fox with blood on its muzzle
can wish on red clover and be a girl again. Little Curio
Lined with the Hearts of Men, the story isn't over. Listen,
the drapes are singing. *Open the window, that the lies may fly out.*

Seven Disappointments (1)

Do not rush to baptize your daughter
in the well. Do not send your seven sons
with a jug. They'll drop it, and you'll curse
them into birds, shoo them into a glass

mountain far from any mention
of their names. When you hear the whir
of wings, do not think of the life you wanted,
but did not have: The lemony sun

pressed on your eyelids, your tree jeweled
with girls to pick and eat. I'll tell you
how it ends: Your daughter will learn
the truth. She will search for her brothers

and bring them home. Maybe this is what
you wanted. But do not give her bread,
a pitcher of water, a little chair. Her guilt
is beyond hunger, thirst, weariness.

And these things will do no good in a world
where children, despite their commonness,
are a delicacy. The sun bares row after row
of serrated teeth. The moon watches,

eyes rolling as if from behind a painting,
and says, *I smell, I smell the flesh of men.*
But the stars give her what you could not:
a way into the mountain, a key

of brittle bone she will only lose.
You might want to look away. She cuts off
her finger and turns it inside the keyhole.
Not everything can be set to music.

The Fortune Teller to the Woodsman

Gaunt and salt-and-pepper as the birches, wolves
are starving in these woods. From here the moon
is a crystal ball. I don't need to look inside

to tell you that if you walk into the trees,
you won't come out. The twigs will just stop

breaking under your boots. The moon backs off,

the later it gets. You could learn a thing or two
from her. Soon she'll be far away, and the tiny
pictures inside will be buzzing lights, like fireflies

in a jar. But I can still swirl my hands around her
and see you in a shock of clover, your bones

gnawed to talc, your wife's shriek filling the forest

so completely, the wolves lap the air for a taste.
Go home and watch the stars bare their small,
shiny teeth. Tonight I've spared you,

but you can't be spared forever. If the moon says
you'll be picked clean, believe her. You'll feed

whatever hunts you the heart hot from your body.

Village Smart

It's what they call the devil, as in *cunning*.
When his cloven heart is hungry, he finds a way to feed it.
For every child sewn up into a sack and drowned,
candy-dipped in pitch, cut and seasoned, there is one
untouched but waiting. Name your first son Sorrowful
if you must. At least you have a son. If the devil comes
to claim him, carve the eyes and tongue from a deer
to prove the deed done. What will you tell your son
about this world? That children can be unzipped
from the bellies of beasts? No one is out of danger.
Darkness threads a needle as fast as light. As the devil eats,
bones pile under the table. Bread cries out in the oven
for fear of burning. A heart nestles among red apples.

SONG OF THE HEIRLOOM APPLE TREE

after Federico Garcia Lorca

Yes, there was always danger. Zeppelins dragged
their shade around the orchard like slow-moving clouds.
Still the sun pinned on us crisp, sweet cameos:
Star Ladies, Pink Pearls, Black Gilliflowers, Mothers.
I'm sure some were flawed, some bruised and soft,
but everything is perfected by distance. Nostalgia clouds
like bloom—that fine, gray dust children shine off
on their sleeves. A hundred years ago, I was promised
an inheritance: turn-of-the-century Golden Drops
glinting like vintage brooches. Instead I am bare.
Cut me down as you did the others. It hurts, but not
as you might expect. I imagine myself a freestone fruit:
The pit clings to the flesh but breaks free easily.

UNCLASSIFIED STARS

1.

One summer, Gretel is sent to live with her grandmother by the sea. We are told that the house is gingerbread. Sugar panes in the windows and so forth. The ocean winds bring sweet, delicious smells from the house down the bluffs. Gulls peck at gumdrops on the sill. In the story, the old woman ties an apron around her middle and brings Gretel cold cups of milk in the mornings. In fact, she wears gypsy scarves and drinks gin over ice. *Darling,* she says, flicking her cigarette and exhaling two lungs worth of dust, *this isn't one of your stories.*

2.

Never mind Grandmother and the liquor and the gulls. The sea is a fact, and its air has edges. Most mornings, Gretel can be found floating on her back in the bay, her small breasts breaking the surface. The pink color of shells. She imagines the candied remains of the eaves dissolving under her tongue.

3.

In the original version, even the sea is a lie. The setting is a forest and Gretel has a brother, Hansel. He shreds bread as they walk to keep track. This, however, is the children's version. It does not account for Gretel's curves, or the way Hansel looks at her under the unclassified stars. He feeds her little pieces of bread with his hands. She takes them into her mouth, nibbling on the tips of his fingers. Life, we've been warned, doesn't taste like it should in stories.

4.

Disregard the part about the bread. It's not that they are lost, but that they keep themselves like a secret. People in town wouldn't understand, but we're better listeners. This is the kind of incest readers champion: cheek to cheek since the womb, sharing a nursery in the formative years. It has always been this way. Gretel and Hansel, Gretel and Hansel. In the picture book, they share open-mouthed kisses in the long shadows, unaware of our eyes.

5.

Ultimately, all revisions of her life collapse into one: the sharpening sea, the candied eaves of the cottage, Hansel's salty fingers in her mouth. At the end of the story, where the moral should be, there are only two nudes reclining, naked and flushed beneath a great oak. Babes in the wood. Who's to say where one ends and the other begins? Where the body forgets its edges. Where the story drops off and calls itself memory, life. Who's to say? They have been rolling so long in the leaves, their two skins smell exactly the same.

Manic Panic

If you lie still and concentrate, you can forget
        your body and float like a balloon to the ceiling

                where plaster stars prick like thumbtacks.
So scoured out, you can't feel anything,

          like the pink-haired girls who butcher their arms.
          Come down. There is no merit badge

for levitation. You can leave your body,
        but it will pucker and fall eventually, snagged

             in bare branches, which like antennae
receive signals too high-pitched for us to hear.

          How sad, everything, and how inexpensive
          to say it out loud. The hills smoke

like a motherboard. Feeling bad has never felt
        better, think the green-haired girls who brand

             the smiles of lighters into their thighs
and wear striped stockings so tight, the stripes distort.

          You're not like them. They're still trying to live
          the days of Manic Panic and bar marquees

where all the *L*s were sevens. How sad, everything,
        and how cheap to say it out loud. The hills smoke

             like mothers, like purple-haired girls.
Stretched taut, filled with nothing, you rise.

Apologue (4)

Érase que se era, en un país muy lejano...

And so it was, in a very distant land, you lay awake
and watched the windows pale until the whole room
was infected with light. Little Black Plum, even in fables
you couldn't sleep. In your last dream, a hundred
years ago, burning swans floated on a lake like votives.
With feathers like wicks, they didn't burn away.
Little Song Best Understood by Children and Animals,
something at their core was indestructible. The smoke
didn't billow, but drifted in neat rings as if from
the captain's cigarillo. Little Rusted Nail, no one
could have predicted the future. You were no prize
for the palm reader. Your hands didn't speak.
They were like pages that had been crumpled up,
and then—on second thought—smoothed out again.
Little Operetta Composed in the Wrong Key, the last
time you slept, swans sailed on the water like a Viking
burial. Every morning, the sun rose and overwhelmed
the east window with flames. If you stayed awake,
Little Tea Leaf, at least you'd know you were burning.
And the story ended. When I find it again, I'll tell it once more.

Suspension

Nothing burns the bridge, and then it burns.

—Terese Svoboda

Once you cross, as you must,
you cannot go back. There is nothing
to retrieve: when the bridge catches fire,

leave it all. Your hair, your hands
may be lit; if you take photographs
into your arms, they too will burn.

You can see the lights of the city
you left behind, but in miniature
from the distance, a diorama.

When the bridge falls, the smoke
of its scaffolding hangs in the air,
burning our eyes. This is architecture

in the new world: the mere shadow
of structure, the suspension bridge
refusing to suspend. To be light

enough to cross, you must be less
of yourself. Remove everything
down to your wristwatch.

Whittle yourself to transparency.
Cross the bridge as it burns, sparks
in the wisps of your hair,

and don't look back.
It is already turning to smoke.
Soon it will not hold you.

2.

...and you will fall into another darkness, one you will find yourself making and remaking until it is perfect.

—Mark Strand

LAST NIGHT ON EARTH

I play Last Night on Earth by closing my eyes
and convincing myself it will all be gone

when I open them: streets lined with pear trees;
crosswalks and people crossing. Waiting
in darkness, I am Pennsylvania dawn before

the sun steamrolls the hills with its flattening
wave of light, before the mist rises off the cows'

shoulders. I am the mist. No, I'm grass so tall,
a child could wade in and never come out.
I am the dime-sized lights blinking at twilight,

calling him inside. No, I am the reedy
imprints on the boy's legs when they find him.

I am the phone ringing in his mother's house
and what is said, the reply to which
is a strangling sound. No, I'm his birthstone

in a pendant she wore, believing it
kept him safe. I am the space inside her

once occupied by that belief. I am the remainder
after loss is equated, the little R beside the zero.
In darkness, I am everything one last time.

No, I am their absence. I am a shrine
to lost streets, trees, crosswalks, crossers.

Oh, I wish the pear trees could stay—
just the pear trees. But if everything is gone,
what could I possibly offer to save them?

Last Night on Earth always ends this way.
Winning means I can't bear to look,

sure the world has dissolved
around me, wondering if I've been spared
because the nothing demands to be seen.

Disenchantment

1.

In the house, he found ears frittering in a hot skillet, teeth
boiling like navy beans, an open bottle of blood's best vintage.
That's when the trouble started. What boy can't tell a beast from
a woman? He should have run for the river, where laundresses
built bridges of cloth, snapping clean, white sheets over the
water. Instead he crawled beneath the quilts, wanting the hair
smoothed back from his forehead. It hardly hurt at all, being
swallowed. He imagined himself a bird in a skirted cage—as if
it were simply nighttime, and in the morning a woman would
come and lift the cloth. *Let my feathers be bathed in light. Let my
feathers be bathed in light.* He repeated until it became a novena.
Without a rosary, he ran his tongue along his teeth, counting
one after the other.

2.

Luckily he's the son of a seamstress. His mother cut him free,
then darned the beast's belly—a black sock turned inside out.
The boy touched each slick tooth to calm his nerves, back and
forth, back and forth. Whole, unharmed, he followed the path
out of the forest. Nets of crows cast themselves onto the trees,
and the boy couldn't pull them down. Each birch was an altar,
each cut an offering: an ear, a finger, hanks of ship-rope hair.
He was both artist and medium, whittling himself as practice
for wood. Leaves flickered and chimed like bells made entirely
of light. Later his mother would say none of it happened. *You're
a fake, a fraud, always remembering things worse than they were.*
Beast or woman? It wasn't clear which had eaten him alive.

3.

It has taken the boy years—*years*—to find the clearing, where a
square rug of sunlight lies on the grass. His mouth is rowed with
numbered prayers, but some of the best parts of him are missing.
Crows grow fat on his scraps. It's all he can do to listen as they rasp
even the morning air to shreds. The child has no business back
there, where the forest canopy interrupts the stars and clouds and
whole columns of light, where beasts and women cannot be told
apart. He is not whole, not unharmed. I don't know how to make
him understand. If he turns fast enough, without warning the trees,
he'll see there is nothing. Everything behind him is gone. I'll make
him say it back to me. *Everything behind me is gone.*

Xenia, 1974

Through the power lines the sky looks like ruled paper.
In this notebook, the pages are filled with birds
someone drew—I can't say it was me—then suddenly
a white sleeve of wind. A cigarette. A pen on the horizon.

From the road we must look like paper dolls—crisp, dark
silhouettes floating through the rooms, rushing to the cellar.
In this strange light, the red barn goes violet, the trees
wear their shadows too close to their skin. A pen

hovers above the horizon, then dips down, as if plowing
our names and the name of this town in deep furrows
until the ink is pressed clean through the paper.
Afterwards everything is rearranged. The ruled page

of the rabbit pen has rabbits drawn in the margins,
fence posts nailed into trees. Blonde strands of scattered
hay gleaming like a girl's hair. In the violet husk of our barn,
in the remains, what voice calls? I can't say it is mine.

Apologue (5)

En la tierra de irás y no volverás…

In a land where you will go but from where you will never return,
Little Black Cricket, you'll follow music inside a mountain
with the other children. Then the rock will be sealed
so that no one can find the door, the stone to push
that might reveal a secret corridor. Little Darning
Needle, you can pray *díos, díos, díos,* but there is no charm
in three—it's just a mnemonic device for the storyteller.
Little Hat the Wind Blew Away, stories begin in light
and end in darkness. Since you are always in darkness,
the tale is lost without its teller. In the world you left,
there is an abacus of birds on a wire, and everyone uses it
to count the missing. *Díos, díos, díos.* Little Twig Snapping
Under the Devil's Shoe, for every crow's heart you swallow
whole, you are promised a gold piece under your tongue.
Now coins fall from your lips when you speak, chiming
around you, but they might as well be pebbles. The pearls
you weep might as well be tears. Little Bride of the Mountain,
there is no more music. No one is coming. When the stone
healed behind you, it sounded like a lid closing over a tomb.
And many years passed. This is the end of all that's given here.

The Well Speaks of Its Own Poison

Not once, but always, there is a woman who cannot allow
another's happiness. She wishes a man dead and means it.

She would eat the eyes of lambs if she believed
they once belonged to him, beheld her rival's body.

She makes me an accessory, filling me *glug glug glug*
with something clear as water, but if I had a throat

of anything but stone, it would burn. Who drinks of me
now will be a tiger, then a wolf, then a roebuck.

Who drinks of me will tear his new love to quilt scraps,
eat himself sick, and flee to a mountain swaddled in fog.

I will not be judged. I've done what I can. To stop the thirsty
from hauling up my bucket, to warn the water-witchers

against divining here, I taught myself to speak. You know
what they say about poisoning a well: Soon it seeps.

Shapeshifter

Half me, you're half haunted.
Your heart is destined to skip
like a scratched record.

But lucky you, you weren't made
of the past, an alchemy that comes out
all rusted. You weren't hauled up

like a car from the lake. No,
you're new. As soon as I memorize
your face, you change it.

Shapeshifter, it's a dream
chase—the more I pursue you,
the faster you run. You answer

my wren with a hawk,
my doe with a fox. The more
you change, the harder it is to

go back. Waking at dawn,
the light outside still limey,
just barely yellow with sunrise,

I hear the first few birds
starting up—one, then another—
then you chiming in: *peep peep peep.*

Half me, I'm half afraid
to see you this morning, wondering
who or what I will find in your bed.

Seven Disappointments (2)

We learn early we're just dots
seen from a great height.

—Amy Gerstler

You are human again, but you remember
both lives. First, a boy's. Swimming
in the green-black lake, sleeping in a loft
with your brothers, having a mother

and father who each time one of you broke
into the world hoped you would be
something else. Seven disappointments,
one for each day of the week. A life you had

but did not want. Then, a bird's. Preening
your blue-black wings, sleeping in a nest
made of spun glass, alighting on your sister,
her arms outstretched like a saint, although

she did not know you then. From the air
everyone you loved was scattered confetti.
The speck of one, the speck of another.
It was a dollhouse view: tiny, varnished

loaves of bread, a miniature candelabra,
book pages the size of postage stamps.
It felt as impossible as your name
on a grain of rice: a life you wanted

but could not keep. Once you watched
the landscape roll beneath you; a movie
of a tree played on the river, its reflection
flickering as if projected. You are human

again, but you will not forget. From the air,
the lit windows of your house looked like
a fallen constellation. There were so many
with no silhouettes to fill them.

FIRST SON

Twelve daughters, and all the woman pines for
is a son. If this one's a boy, she tells her husband,

the girls must go. She carves twelve coffins,
sews twelve little death pillows, stuffs each one

with the dark curls that fall to the floor
when she cuts the girls' hair. The man can't bear

the risk, so he sends his girls into the wilderness.
If it's safe to return, they'll see smoke

curling above the trees, smell their baby
locks burning. But a boy child is born

and bathed in sweet milk each morning.
Later the child discovers twelve coffins in the cellar,

yellowed pillows full of hair the same shade
as his own. How can he live, knowing

what was done in his name? What was nearly done?
He curses his mother, half forgives his father,

hunts his sisters to the hollows of faraway trees.
But he's too late. They've flown beyond the world

of mercy and forgiveness, the human world.
They aren't girls anymore but wild, winged

creatures, their eyes black as the eyes of crows.

THAW

When I turn off the lamp, the room is lit
by birds. Hundreds are frozen in the trees

as if encrusted in sugar, their feathers
crystallized, beaks frosted shut,

each open eye a dark, glittering gumdrop.
Come thaw, they'll pry themselves

from these limbs and leave, unfastening
their candied eyes from me. But tonight

I'm frozen in their gaze. Their bodies
bathe me in a cool, sweet light. I lie

awake and listen as the rain begins—
water gnawing at a harder form of itself.

Apologue (6)

Había una vez, en los tiempos del rey que rabió…

Once upon a time, in the times of the angry king,
a woman gave her hand to a wolf. Little View from a Lit
Ferris Wheel, you know better than to marry anything
that could clamp its jaws on you. How would he sing
your babies to sleep? The moon tugs on his throat
like a tide, but nothing else will do. Little Window
into the Future, the bride learned this soon enough.
When he howled, thousands of birds hid in the hearts
of trees. Their electric cries no longer crackled and sparked
across invisible wires. The bride did not forget their songs.
Little Wall I Hit My Head Upon, don't marry. How would
anyone keep you? Love is a disease not easily cured.
In this story, the wolf left his bride alone, but he wanted
to keep a close watch. Do you know this part, Little Patch
of Bloodstained Snow? He cut out the eyes of calves
and arranged them around her. But the gaze was useless;
nothing was behind it. *Hush now and be still,* the birds
showed the bride, hiding in their hollows. She waited
for the eyes to cloud over and rot. Little Sip of Chartreuse,
she outlasted the looking. *And she lived well, to the end of her days.*

The Shepherd's Horn

Shame on us for thinking anything
we do goes unseen: If you kill a man,
it will always come to light. If you bury
your brother under a bridge, no matter

how deep, his white bones will surface
like broken shells on a beach. It will be
a bright morning—the wind will have
scoured everything clean while you slept,

scrubbing every cloud from the sky—
when a shepherd finds one bone
and carves a mouthpiece for his horn.
And soon he'll see that the bone sings

on its own. It sings your name, murderer.
When the shepherd plays, it sounds like
someone pleading. Shame on us for
thinking we can suppress the truth:

The bones tell their body's story to
the bloody end. If you bury them again,
they'll sing in the ground. If you toss them
into the waves, they'll sing in the sea.

If you cover your ears, the bones will
sing inside you, as clear as the voice that
lives in your own head. Listen, murderer.
No one said the music is beautiful.

No one said the shepherd enjoys playing
this haunted song that scares the children.
What did you expect? The truth is not
melodic, not something to dance to.

LANTERNS

The stories say the banished dead are wild now,
crouching among scrawny trees, skinning rabbits
and raising them like lanterns. Who needs light
when you're disfigured, kept from even the idea
of heaven, with slit throats or bulging eyes or
bits of skull clinging like pieces of seashell.
The stories say they have no hearts. That they wear
the broken bodies they left in. They can't be
whole again, but at least they can stay in the woods,
under the creek bridge. At least they can lick dew
from leaves until their tongues rust. At least
if the creek runs, it will keep them from seeing
their reflections, their eyes too haunted to be the eyes
of deer. The stories say that you can hear them.
That they sing by the lanterns of skinned rabbits.
That the music is what coats the grass with frost.

WHITE

Winter, suddenly, and so much
whiteness aches to the roots
of our hair. My eyes

open and close, oysters.
Every scrap of wretched sleep
says there are no pearls inside.

But who knows how white
our bones are. Untouched,
they may be timid or

they gleam from time in darkness.
Their fluorescent hum
keeps insomniacs company.

I hadn't realized their song
inside the body is a round,
repeating: *white, white, white.*

Hush Now

My head was cloudy,
not transparent

as the plastic body
in the children's wing

of the museum,
but free of charge

you could still push
rows of multicolored

buttons and watch
pain register in the gray

knot of my brain.
Neurons lit up neon

in the parcels of my skull.
To keep calm as I felt

flashing, flashing
behind my eyes,

I memorized beat-up
jeans, six pearly snaps

on my cowgirl shirt,
the sky blanched

cigarette white. Then
I pulsed like a strobe,

like seizure. *Hush now
and run,* light hissed

inside the hot coils.
Run as fast as you can.

Yes, I said, shorting,
still lit. *Then what.*

Apologue (7)

Dicen los que lo vieron—yo no estaba, pero me lo dijeron...

Those who saw it say—I wasn't there, but they told me
the mourning dove severed her tail, and not even flour paste
could make her whole again. Little Moth-Eaten Cardigan,
we must depend on bodies that rot. Little Cavity
Pining for Sweetness, it's hopelessly counterintuitive:
We lock our doors and hide gold coins under our eyelids,
but the only thing of worth is there for the taking.
It's like keeping your heart in a hatbox. Little Mailbox
Without a Letter to Warm It, this gnawing of teeth
is not a lullaby. It can't sing you to sleep. What world
do you think this is? There is more to fear in this body
than anywhere. Forget the wolves, the monsters that pass
for men, the clumsy undead stumbling across the field.
Little Key on a Velvet Cord, bad things happen no matter
how good you are. Every morning your jaw aches with them.
When the body's gone, we have nowhere to live.
This is the end of the story. I told it just like they told it to me.

If I Forget to Tell You

If I forget to tell you, daughter, keep your head
if your hands are severed: you can still eat pears

straight from the tree with your mouth.
If your hands are severed, wear silver

fists until your new ones bud in spring. Keep these
shining charms to remind you how fruit tastes

when you're bleeding. Daughter, don't believe
there is always a place for you—an empty cottage,

as if the person living there wandered off
and lost his way back. You might think

your skull is like a library, where each moment
is catalogued and waiting. Daughter, I believed it.

Then autumn was pulled down behind me
like a cheap picture studio backdrop

of fallen leaves, everything rusted. If I forget
to tell you, choose a word and let it live

alone in your mouth a while. *Pears, pears, pears.*
Sometimes there isn't room for more. Daughter,

where silence is permitted to grow, it grows.

WHICH SONG, WHICH CRICKET

after Gabriela Mistral

I began as one cricket singing
one song. Soon we were all singing.
The dusk was unintelligible.

I hadn't moved, but suddenly I was lost.
Which song is my song? Which cricket am I?

I will never be one cricket again.
I could wait for midnight's silences
and try to fill them. I could stop singing

and listen to the little me-shaped hole
torn in the roaring twilight. The sound

of me missing might be clearer
than my song. I could gift it to the night,
which misses its dear, departed silences.

Even the stars quiver on their own
high frequency. I'm sure they're lost, too.

FUNDEVOGEL

Never leave me, and I will never leave you.

If I lost you in the Schwarzwald,
I'm not sure I could bring you back.
These deep Germanic woods, stinking
of bear fur, half the footpaths grown over,

have their own rules. If I turn away for
one moment, a hawk could swoop down
and carry you high into a treetop. You'd be
long-lost. Babe in the wood, you so love

the trees, you must have some bird in you.
Even in the Black Forest, slack orange
tulips fallen from poplars are beautiful
enough to eat—seemingly sugared,

as if off a cake. My tow-headed,
rosy-cheeked girl, you've been fattened
on happiness, mother's milk,
mother love. You'd make some witch

quite a treat. So let me carry you.
We'll sing to stay awake, keeping one eye
on the trees. Maybe as long as we are
touching, nothing can harm us.

Lights, Lemons

There were lights in the lemon trees
so you could see the lemons.

There were lights in the lemon trees
and a whistle for calling out.

There was a girl among the lit lemons
who blew the whistle and waited

for someone, anyone, to find her.
There were lights in the lemon trees

and a whistle and a girl and no one,
no one came when she called.

Always the girl is a version of you.
I wonder what whistle I could give,

what pitch I could listen for
in all those leaves and lit fruit,

so I could come and lift you
down into the dark grass.

THE DARK

Nothing to fear, the dark outside the window
is yours. It didn't just blow in with the rain tonight.

It doesn't migrate in a *V*-shaped arrow pointing south.
You're the only company it keeps, the only language

it understands. The dark knows your scent and the rasp
of your breathing. When you move, it moves with you.

But don't mistake loyalty for love; it doesn't love you—
no more than the shadow stitched to your feet.

I know it well, your dark, descended from my own.
The day you were born, I clipped a bit of mine

and fed it to you—dark, milk, and tears. Nothing
to fear, it's yours now. It will never get full, a black

envelope you can slip anything inside. Like the moon
or a mother, it's there when it's not. No matter

where you are, it will fog the pane with its breath.
Whenever the dark arrives, it comes home.

Apologue (8)

Al fin de los tiempos, el viento triste dice todo...

At the end of time, the sad wind says everything
left on its breath. Little Stick of Kindling, you lie
awake, expecting word. Each night stars arrive
like letters from the dead, never addressed but somehow
delivered. Little Daughter of Gypsies, the postman rides
his horse to the end of the earth, only to find a hole
in the bottom of his satchel, a tear in the sky where
the constellation was pinned. Little Song to the Tune
of "Greensleeves," whatever light we receive is long gone.
The sad wind shakes the stars from their branches.
They fall, blazing, like golden apples. Little Cheek Flushed
with Fever, fill your apron with them. Some are snarled
in your black hair, some hiss into the sea. You can find
lit places fathoms down, bright as an overexposed
photograph taken on your street at night. Little Fruit
Fallen from the Heavens, those lights will burn out.
Dusk is darkness held at arm's length. Now you see
how much the end of time resembles the beginning.
This story entered in a silver trail and came out golden.

I THINK OF YOU, ERÉNDIRA

after Gabriel García Márquez

I was in love. Everything glass I touched turned blue.
Every orange I opened revealed a diamond. Somewhere
a cricket played and played. The trees dimmed their lights
so gradually, I hardly noticed. What I mean is that I loved

everything. Everyone knew from the blue vases, the blue
figurines. From oranges hiding jewels you could crack
a tooth on. From the cricket's music chipping away
the air between us. From darkness verging slowly
as the trees lowered their lights. I was in love

with everything then. Even my windows went blue
as sca glass, and through them so did the streets,
the bicycles, the birds. The view startled like a diamond
inside an orange. One night the cricket finished boring
through the air to me. But before I could see him,
the trees went dark and took me with them.

NOTES

The "Apologues" owe a debt to *Tales Our Abuelitas Told: A Hispanic Folktale Collection* by F. Isabel Campoy and Alma Flor Ada (Atheneum, 2006). For each poem, the Spanish epigraph is a common opening line in a traditional folktale, and the poem's first line is that epigraph translated into English. The final italicized line of these poems is an English translation of a common closing line in folktales.

"The List of Dangers": The italicized phrase in stanza six is quoted from Eliot Solomon, 2004.

"Notes on Camp" was inspired by *This American Life*, Episode 109: Notes on Camp, which originally aired in August 1998 on National Public Radio.

"Seven Disappointments (1)": The italicized material in stanza six is from "The Seven Ravens" by Jacob and Wilhelm Grimm in *The Complete Grimm's Fairy Tales* (Pantheon, 2006).

"Apologue (4)": Line seven is based on a quote by Igor Stravinsky.

"Which Song, Which Cricket": The italicized questions in stanza two are from *Crickets and Frogs: A Fable* by Gabriela Mistral, translated and adapted by Doris Dana (Atheneum, 1972).

"Fundevogel": The epigraph is from "Fundevogel" by Jacob and Wilhelm Grimm in *The Complete Grimm's Fairy Tales* (Pantheon, 2006).

"Lights, Lemons" is for—and thanks to—Violet Smith-Beehler.

"I Think of You, Eréndira" owes a debt to *Innocent Eréndira and Other Stories* by Gabriel García Márquez (Perennial, 1979).

63

Acknowledgments

Thanks to the editors of the following journals in which the following poems first appeared, sometimes in slightly different versions or with different titles:

Blackbird: "Seven Disappointments (2)"
The Brooklyn Review: "Disenchantment"
Crab Orchard Review: "Notes on Camp"
Cream City Review: "Apologue (6)" and "The Shepherd's Horn"
failbetter.com: "The Fortune Teller to the Woodsman," "Hush Now,"
     "Manic Panic," and "Suspension"
The Florida Review: "The List of Dangers"
The Gettysburg Review: "Apologue (3)" and "Apologue (8)"
Gulf Coast: "Game" and "Xenia, 1974"
Indiana Review: "An Island in the Movies" and "Vanishing Point"
Jabberwock Review: "Mental Note"
The Laurel Review: "Apologue (4)"
The Massachusetts Review: "Apologue (1)" and "Apologue (2)"
Mid-American Review: "Ohio," "Unclassified Stars," "Village Smart," and
     "The Well Speaks of Its Own Poison"
New Ohio Review: "The Dark" and "Lanterns"
The Paris Review: "Apologue (5)"
Quarterly West: "Seven Disappointments (1)"
Salamander: "Lights, Lemons"
Sweet: "Fundevogel," "If I Forget to Tell You," and "Song of the Heirloom
     Apple Tree"
the tiny: "Freedom Colony"
Third Coast: "I Think of You, Eréndira" and "Last Night on Earth"
Tupelo Quarterly: "Apologue (7)," "First Son," "Shapeshifter," and "Which
     Song, Which Cricket"

Several of these poems also appear in a chapbook, *The List of Dangers* (Kent State University Press, 2010).

"Village Smart" was reprinted in *The Year's Best Fantasy & Horror 2008* (St. Martin's Griffin, 2008).

"Manic Panic" was reprinted online in the 2008 *Best of the Net Anthology* (Sundress Publications, 2008).

Many thanks to the National Endowment for the Arts and the Ohio Arts Council for their generous support. Thanks also to Stanley Plumly, Katie Pierce, Linda Gregerson, Amy Gerstler, Lesley Jenike, Maggie Anderson, Kelly McGuinness, Su Blackwell, Matthew Zapruder, Betsy Wheeler, Bob Flanagan, and Kathy Fagan. And more than thanks to my husband, Jason Beehler.

Finally and especially, to Jeffrey Levine, Jim Schley, Marie Gauthier, Ann Aspell, and everyone at Tupelo Press, and to Kimiko Hahn for selecting this book from so many worthy manuscripts, I am grateful beyond words.

OTHER BOOKS FROM TUPELO PRESS

Fasting for Ramadan: Notes from a Spiritual Practice (memoir),
Kazim Ali

Another English: Anglophone Poems from Around the World (anthology),
edited by Catherine Barnett and Tiphanie Yanique

The Vital System (poems), CM Burroughs

Stone Lyre: Poems of René Char, translated by Nancy Naomi Carlson

Living Wages (poems), Michael Chitwood

Gossip and Metaphysics: Russian Modernist Poems and Prose,
edited by Katie Farris, Ilya Kaminsky, and Valzhyna Mort

Or, Gone (poems), Deborah Flanagan

The Posthumous Affair (novel), James Friel

Entwined: Three Lyric Sequences (poems), Carol Frost

Poverty Creek Journal (memoir), Thomas Gardner

The Faulkes Chronicle (novel), David Huddle

Darktown Follies (poems), Amaud Jamaul Johnson

A God in the House: Poets Talk About Faith (interviews),
edited by Ilya Kaminsky and Katherine Towler

Phyla of Joy (poems), Karen An-hwei Lee

New Cathay: Contemporary Chinese Poetry (anthology),
edited by Ming Di

Lucky Fish (poems), Aimee Nezhukumatathil

The Infant Scholar (poems), Kathy Nilsson

Ex-Voto (poems), Adélia Prado, translated by Ellen Doré Watson

Intimate: An American Family Photo Album (memoir), Paisley Rekdal

Thrill-Bent (novel), Jan Richman

Vivarium (poems), Natasha Sajé

Cream of Kohlrabi (stories), Floyd Skloot

The Perfect Life (essays), Peter Stitt

Soldier On (poems), Gale Marie Thompson

Swallowing the Sea (essays), Lee Upton

Lantern Puzzle (poems), Ye Chun